AROUND THE GLOBE MUST SEE PLACES IN AFRICA

Africa is the world's second-largest and second-most-populous continent. Africa host a large diversity of ethnicities, cultures and languages. Africa is the world's hottest continent with deserts and drylands covering 60% of land surface area. Megafauna like giraffe, zebra, gorilla, hippopotamus, chimpanzee and wildebeest are unique to the continent and only found here.

GIZA NECROPOLIS

is an archaeological site on the Giza Plateau, on the outskirts of Cairo, Egypt. This complex of ancient monuments includes the three pyramid complexes known as the Great Pyramids, the massive sculpture known as the Great Sphinx, several cemeteries, a workers' village and an industrial complex. The pyramid is estimated to have around 2,300,000 stone blocks that weigh from 2 to 30 tons each and there are even some blocks that weigh over 50 tons.

MOUNT KILIMANJARO

is the highest mountain in Africa and the highest free-standing mountain in the world. Almost every kind of ecological system is found on the mountain: cultivated land, rain forest, heath, moorland, alpine desert and an arctic summit. Approximately 25,000 people attempt to summit Mt. Kilimanjaro annually. Approximately two-thirds are successful. Altitude-related problems is the most common reason climbers turn back.

ABU SIMBEL TEMPLES

are two massive rock temples at Abu Simbel , a village in Nubia, southern Egypt. One temple is dedicated to King Ramses II, and the second temple is dedicated to his beloved wife Queen Nefertari. The complex is part of the UNESCO World Heritage Site known as the Nubian Monuments. The complex was relocated in its entirety in 1968, on an artificial hill made from a domed structure, high above the Aswan High Dam reservoir.

VICTORIA FALLS

is a waterfall in southern Africa on the Zambezi River at the border of Zambia and Zimbabwe. By the end of the 1990s almost 300,000 people were visiting the falls annually. A famous feature is the naturally formed "Armchair" (now sometimes called "Devil's Pool"), a natural pool at the edge of Victoria Falls that is occasionally safe for swimming.

VALLEY OF THE KINGS

is a valley in Egypt where, for a period of nearly 500 years from the 16th to 11th century BC, tombs were constructed for the Pharaohs and powerful nobles of the New Kingdom. There are over 60 tombs in the Valley of the Kings. The most famous tomb in the Valley of the Kings is that of the Pharaoh Tutankhamun, sometimes called King Tut.

VIRUNGA MOUNTAINS

are a chain of volcanoes in East Africa, along the northern border of Rwanda, the Democratic Republic of the Congo and Uganda. The name "Virunga" is an English version of the Kinyarwanda word ibirunga, which means "volcanoes". Apart from their spectacular beauty, the forests of these mountains form the last remaining home of the highly endangered Mountain Gorilla.

SERENGETI NATIONAL PARK

is a Tanzanian national park in the Serengeti ecosystem in the Mara and Simiyu regions. The park covers 14,750 square kilometres of grassland plains, savanna, riverine forest, and woodlands. The region hosts the largest mammal migration in the world and is a popular destination for African safaris.